D1590334

ANIMAL SUFFERING

AND

THE HOLOCAUST:

The Problem With Comparisons

Roberta Kalechofsky

Micah Publications, Inc

Printed in the United States of America

ISBN: 0-916288-49-8

micah publications,inc
www. micahbooks.com

...We pray each night that we will have
A history. We pray for all that is uninvented.

From "Intellectual Beauty," by Baron Wormser

INTRODUCTION

The Jews are not a metaphor for anyone else.
They're their own people. Cynthia Ozick

Many years ago, Harry Slochower, with whom I then was taking a course on modern European literature, gave me the lens through which I thereafter regarded individuals and history: "Every difference is a difference." The sentence is limpidly simple, almost silly simple, but like many such statements, surprisingly profound. It constitutes a corrective to the natural tendency of the cognitive mind to think through metaphors and comparisons, to make connections which erase distinctions, to veer towards tidy equations. If "A is to B, as B is to Z, then A must be like Z, or even be Z" However, every difference *is* a difference, genetically and historically. We may say that both Alexander the Great and Adolf Hitler shared the ambition to be a world conqueror, but the comparison ends there because history will not support much further connection.

Not only are human beings different from animals, but animals are different from each other. "The animal kingdom," is not an amorphous realm of non-human creatures. An elephant may share genetic material with a frog, but an elephant is not a frog. Human beings may share 98% or more of their genetic

5

code with chimpanzees, but human beings are not chimpanzees. This is not a derogation of the principle of equality, but an observation that the world is not populated on the principle of equality, but on the principle of differences and otherness. In his book, *The Outermost House,* the naturalist, Henry Beston, wrote,

"The animal shall not be measured by man. In a world older and more complete than ours, they move finished and complete, gifted with extensions of the senses we have lost or never attained, living by voices we shall never hear. They are not brethren, they are not underlings; they are other nations, caught with ourselves in the net of life and time, fellow prisoners of the splendour and travail of the earth."

Many religions have rich traditions concerning animals, but these traditions have mostly lapsed in a secular world, and we do not know how applicable they ever were. Some Christian reformers like John Wesley in the eighteenth century, called for the cessation of bloodsports and cruelty towards animals in England, on the principle of reverence for God's creatures, though animal rights reformers in the mid-eighteenth century did not regard animals as their equal. The eighteenth century English cleric, Humphrey Primatt, who wrote one of the first books to argue the rights of animals on religious and moral grounds, regularly referred to animals as "our lesser brethren," yet gave the modern animal rights movement one of its battle cries: "Pain is pain no matter who suffers it." This is a truism which others who wish to obliterate *all* distinction between humans and animals would like to forget. If it is true that humans are obviously different from leopards, frogs and mice, it is also true that we share with them the horror of death, extinction, pain, fear of starvation; sexual appetite; and with many animals maternal bonding and altruistic and social instincts. Most suffering today, whether of animals or humans, suffering beyond calculation, whether it is physiological or the

6

ripping apart of mother and offspring, is at the hands of other humans. Pain is a curse, and gratuitous pain inflicted by humans on other humans or on animals is evil.

Comparison between animals and humans and speculation about their relationship in "the great chain of being" was part of philosophical thought for millennia, but went into decline as the Western world became urbanized, divorced from animal life, and degraded the position of animals, without elevating much of human life. The seventeenth century philosopher Descartes shot the first volley in degrading both animal and human life when he declared animals to be machines. It was immediately and darkly apprehended by some contemporary philosophers that if one could interpret animals as machines, one could interpret humans as machines, for the fact is that neither philosophy nor science can draw precise boundaries between animals and humans. As the animal became subjected to the rigors of the laboratory for medical purposes, the human body came to be viewed more and more as a machine. The Nazis were the first (but not the only) to subject both animals and humans to the same task of yielding answers to diseases, when they caged apes and humans side by side in Buchenwald to study the ravages of typhus.

The machine metaphor has had some advantages for modern medicine, but the metaphor also has dark implications for the human race. If we learn how to cure disease by experimenting on animals, we also learn how to destroy life by refining weapons of mass destruction on animals; how to transform animals into machines; and ultimately how to transform humans into machines. Rodney A. Brooks predicts in his book, *Flesh and Machines,* that it is only a matter of time before humans will become robots. The classic argument about the distinction between humans and animals has been replaced by the problem of distinction between humans and machines. It is in the experimental laboratory that rat and human come so

7

close as almost to breathe into each other's souls. As Guido Ceronetti in *The Silence of the Body* observes, human life is measured by the rat in the experimental setting we hold so dear.

"...I wonder to what extent humanity, incurably *healed* by Western medicine, is now trapped by the rats it exterminates with such ingenious nonchalance in its laboratories....In most, why not say all, prescriptions, the hand that writes is inspired by a rat....Today the rat nibbles at us from the depths of its unnatural suffering, from its tiny lazarettos of certain, excruciating death."

Those who decry the loss of distinction between humans and animals should note that medical research asserts an equivalence, if not equality, between animals and humans for the purpose of doing research. Yet often animal research has to yield to the differences between humans and animals because differences are eventually cumulative. Eventually they add up to a different species, a different trajectory through biological and historical time, and a different history. Human history may be shaped by biological contingencies, but it is not defined by them.

If, as Henry Beston wrote, "The animal shall not be measured by man," should humans be measured by animals, should their travails, their appetites, their longings, their failures, their disappointments, their crises, be measured by animals? Human life cannot be measured by animal life anymore than the frog's life and needs can be measured by the elephant's. We must pay attention to what all life holds in common as well as by what it does not hold in common, and construct a philosophy of justice which takes into account differences as well as similarities.

A radical difference between animals and humans is that humans are text creatures, and this is as true of preliterate and illiterate societies who hand their texts down orally, as it is of literate societies. Human beings are creatures whose histories are transmuted into symbols and texts, who become identified and self-identified with them. Photographs stripped of meaningful text are brute indexes to reality. As Susan Sontag writes in her study of war photographs, *Regarding The Pain of Others,* photographs are the modern counterpart to sound bites. She points out in her examination of a century of horrific photographs of war, of bodies ripped apart by cannon, of faces blown off, of soldiers lying with their entrails spilling out, such photographs have not brought an end to war. Nor is it clear how viewers view such photographs, how they view the pain of others. Indeed, the cover to her book shows a man hanging and another man langorously gazing at him. The one who gazes is not moved by what he gazes at; he gazes at leisure, a relaxed, almost sumptuous leisure. The gaze is morally vacuous. The difference between this gaze and the limp hanging body horrifies. How can anyone look upon pain so unmoved? Yet her book gives evidence that many people do, some even look with satisfaction, with schadenfreude, with the perennial interest that grotesquery invites and which might even encourage voyeurism. "Not all reactions to pictures are under the supervision of reason and conscience. Most depictions of the tormented, mutilated bodies do arouse a prurient interest."

Much of the human race has an appetite for the grotesque, as Sontag points out: there is "an innate tropism towards the gruesome," and like it or not "...love of cruelty is as natural to human beings as is sympathy."

A photograph may invite different reactions at different times, in different cultures. A world such as ours which feasts on shock, may be inured to shock, may not have a moral reaction to photographs of animals and human beings being burned or experimented upon. The literary critic, Frank Kermode, remarked that "shock is the least durable of esthetic responses." In a culture such as ours saturated with shock imagery, suffering from collective attention deficit disorder,

9

shock may also be the least durable of intellectual and moral responses.

More crucially, Sontag remarks that "This remembering through photographs eclipses other forms of understanding and remembering....Harrowing photographs do not inevitably lose their power to shock. But they are not much help if the task is to understand. Narratives can make us understand. Photographs do something else: they haunt us." But they do not necessarily bring understanding or reform. A century and more of harrowing war photographs have not brought an end to war.

Tzvetan Todorov, who reviewed Sontag's book in *The New Republic* (April 21 and 28, 2003) reiterates the point: "...a photograph can stun us, but taken out of context it may not convey any significant meaning....images are subjects without predicates; they invoke the world intensely, but they do not tell us, of themselves, what we should think about it." Imagine the following: we see a sheep hanging by his neck; we see a man hanging by his neck; we see a black man hanging by his neck; we see a man with a yellow star hanging by his neck; we see a man with a pink triangle hanging by his neck; we see a pregnant woman hanging by her neck; we see a child hanging by his neck. We see a pig being roasted; we see a woman being burned at a stake; we see a black man whose body has been burned and hung.

We can easily assume the cause for the animal's being hung or roasted, but what do we know of why the humans are being hung or burned? Without narrative to explain the witch hunts of the 16th and 17th centuries, or the five centuries of the Inquisition, or the lynching of African Americans, or the Holocaust, what do the human hanging bodies mean to us? Labelling the photographs do not compensate for the vacuity of narrative. To see a photograph, no matter how grotesque is, as Sontag points out, to dismiss the history and politics which distinguish these human deaths.

When historical material is transferred out of its original context, it usually changes, and those who lived those events lose control over the telling of their history. This is the danger in comparing the Holocaust to abortion or to the production of meat, or comparing the lynching of African Americans to hanging an animal, or the roasting of an animal to the centuries of auto da fé in which men and women were burned at the stake. Jews are and should be sensitive to the transference of Jewish history into other contexts: much has been taken from them and often ends being used against them, perhaps not always by those who originally took the material, but cultural material and symbols are fluid and hard to control.

PETA's campaign, "Holocaust on Your Plate," is not the first effort to compare an episode of cruel human history with cruelty towards animals. In 1988, Marjorie Spiegel's book, *The Dreaded Comparison: Human and Animal Slavery* (Preface by Alice Walker) revealed important parallels in the abuse of humans and animals, as does Charles Patterson's book, *Eternal Treblinka.* What both demonstrate is that often what is first practised on animals is eventually done to humans. (Ancient cultures taught their young warriors the "manliness" of war by first sending them out to hunt.) What gives Spiegel's book resonance is the accompanying texts, which bring to the history of the African slave trade a perspective not to be found elsewhere.

If photographs have such a poor record of reform, as Sontag's book suggests, what then of the Holocaust Museum in Washington, DC, and elsewhere? To begin with, Holocaust museums do not aim at reform, which is the purpose of PETA's campaign. Holocaust museums aim at bearing witness and remembering. They are places of sorrow, not of protest. The photographs in the Holocaust Museum in Washington, DC, as in Yad Vashem, are buttressed with a plethora of narrative text which attempt to explain the Holocaust as a culmination of history, politics, theology, and social forces. They are places of research and of history. Most important, as Sontag observes, "they invoke the miracle of survival."

The Holocaust has acquired an iconic place in Jewish history and Jewish memory. The PETA exhibit tears it out of that context and to many Jews deracinates its meaning. There is connective tissue between animal suffering and the Holocaust: aspects are joined together particularly in the industrial age, in the tendency in the modern era to institutionalize evil on a vast scale, to enact it and rationalize it with scientific momentum. But animal suffering and the Holocaust fall into different historical frameworks, and comparison between them aborts the historic matrix and force of anti-Semitism.

If photographs per se do not work, what does work to focus the public's attention on cruel institutions? If we had to assign a single event that turned the tide in the Abolitonist movement, it was a literary work, *Uncle Tom's Cabin.* But timing of the book was also important. Published fifty years earlier, it might have had little impact. Photographs have another desperate limitation. Unfortunately, they cannot uncover the corrosive effect of willful ignorance in which the public colludes with evil institutions and then, like Pilate, pretends innocence and washes its hands of all knowledge.

Roberta Kalechofsky
Spring, 2003

1 2

Animal Suffering And The Holocaust

It's only an experiment, an experiment. Not a judgment
of poison for poison

From"In the Laboratory," by Dan Pagis

John Vyvyan complained in his book, *In Pity and In Anger,* (1969) that the cruelties of the animal research community are so enormous that those who seek to expose them are accused of exaggeration:

> One of the difficulties in presenting the case against the cruelty of science is that it is too good to be credible. Writers who have told the truth have always been accused of exaggeration; and those who have striven to cloak and defend these things, by persuasive and persistent lies, have been believed. In point of fact, exaggeration is hardly possible, and only a minute fraction of these enormities will ever be made known....our aim is to tell a truth about modern society so shameful that it cannot be imparted in a felicitous style. (p. 133).

Telford Taylor, Chief Counsel for the Prosecution of the Nazi doctors, had the same problem at the Nuremberg trials in what has become known as *The Medical Case.* He stated that his task was to prove that "these incredible events be established by clear and public proof; so that no one can ever doubt that they were fact and not fable...." (*Dark Face of Science*, p. 157). John Vyvyan asks: "But to whom were such events 'incredible?' They were of a kind that had been predicted often enough. They could not have been incredible to anyone conversant with the history of vivisection....They were incredible only to people who had chosen to be blind." (Ibid., p. 158).

It is difficult for unspeakable cruelty to be assimilated to the psychical framework of most humans, it is hazardous to our necessary belief that human nature for the most part is trustworthy; so we label unspeakable cruelties as aberrant behavior. But the "shameful truth" about modern medicine is that it is not aberrant, but systemic; it has been the daily work of researchers who have been trained for a hundred and fifty years to ignore conscience until conscience atrophied. Now we have the serious, perhaps insurmountable problem, that this amoral force has power over war, health, our daily lives, our cellular and genetic make-up. In *The Silence of the Body,* Guido Ceronetti stakes out the dimensions of this problem: "Given the impossibility of forcing medicine back inside moral boundaries, thought, the assailant, strives to *understand* its terrifying object...." (p. 225-226)

Medicine achieved this power in the animal research laboratories, verifying the premise of the nineteenth century physiologists that the purpose of vivisection was to surmount the problems of conscience and morality by reducing a sentient creature to an object. The Nazis learned the lesson. As James Glass point out, "...this process of denying the body or corporeality is a powerful political theme." It was a powerful theme with Descartes, a powerful theme in the game plan of the nineteenth century physiologists, and a powerful theme in the

1 5

Nazi regime. The connective evidence is brutal, but the animal research community depends on the good will of ordinary people not to attend to brutal facts. In *Alternative Experiments to Experiments on Animals*, Dr. Dallas Pratt accused those who refuse to look at the evidence of animal suffering in the laboratories to be guilty of moral sloth. In addition to the practice of secrecy on the part of the animal researchers and the public's trust in scientists, moral sloth allows this brutal evil to continue.

With respect to suffering, the world today is the same vale of tears described by psalmists and poets for millennia. With respect to suffering, pain, cruelty, and the ineptness of the human race to furnish even a modicum of ease for most human beings, nothing has changed. In the West, technology distances us from the famine, starvation, disease and poverty that is the common lot of most human beings, and most human beings everywhere are indifferent to the hideous suffering of the animal world, most of which is not inflicted by nature "red in tooth and claw," but by humans themselves. Besides the daily hideous pain of laboratory animals and those in slaughterhouses, other categories of animal suffering are innumerable, often inflicted for frivolous reasons of entertainment, fashion, imagined sexual enhancement or, as Plutarch said eighteen hundred years ago, "for a little taste upon the tongue." Take the Chinese trade in bile from the gallbladder of black bears who are captured and confined in cages so small the bears cannot stand up or move about in them. Condemned to sit or crouch for years, bile is drained daily from their bodies to be sold on the market for medicine. The supposed need for their bile does not explain the meanness of their cramped cages. Take the hideous paté de foie gras industry, practised in France, Israel, and elsewhere, where geese are force fed with plungers pushed down their gullets until their livers burst within them for "a little taste upon the tongue" of those who sit in fancy restaurants and shop in gourmet markets; take the Korean delight in dogs who are strangled

16

slowly in the belief that terror makes the adrenaline flow in their tortured bodies and enhances the taste of their meat.

Such views and practices were prevalent in the West two centuries ago. In her book, *A Natural History of the Senses*, Diane Ackerman writes,

> Some of the strangest culinary habits arose in England during the eighteenth century....the idea arose that torturing animals made its meat healthier and better tasting ...people indulged in ghoulish preparations that turned their kitchens into charnel houses. They chopped up live fish, which they claimed made the flesh firmer, they tortured bulls before killing them, because they said the meat would otherwise be unhealthy; they tenderized pigs and calves by whipping them to death with knotted ropes; they hung poultry upside down and slowly bled them to death; they skinned living animals.

Recipe books included descriptions of how to beat a chicken to death. Diane Ackerman records *The Cook's Oracle* by Dr. William Kitchiner who unashamedly gave this following description of how to roast a goose or a duck:

> Take a Goose, or a Duck, or some such lively creature, pull off all her feathers, only the head and neck must be spared: then make a fire round about her, not too close to her, that the smoke do not choak her, and that the fire may not burn her too soon; not too far off, that she may not escape free; within the circle of the fire let there be set small cups and pots of water, wherin salt and honey are mingled; and let there be set also chargers full of sodden Apples, cut into small pieces in the dish. The Goose must be all larded, and basted over with butter: put then fire about her, but do not make too

much haste, when as you see her begin to roast; for by walking about and flying here and there, being cooped in by the fire that stops her way out the wearied Goose is kept in; she will fall to drink the water to quench her thirst, and cool her heart, and all her body, and the Apple sauce will make her dung and cleanse and empty her. And when she roasteth, and consumes inwardly, always wet her head and heart with a wet sponge; and when you see her giddy with running, and begin to stumble, her heart wants moisture, and she is roasted enough. Take her up and set her before your guests and she will cry as you cut off any part from her and will be almost eaten up before she be dead: it is mighty pleasant to behold!

Picture the salivating diners, fork and knife in hand, lust swarming through their mouths for that little taste upon the tongue, cutting into the duck whose heart is still beating.

Nor do these horrors outdo the modern, mechanized slaughterhouses of the West where cruelty is a byproduct of efficiency, of the demanding, unceasing movement of the assembly killing line, and the inevitable sadism that creeps in. Gail Eisnitz' book, *Slaughterhouse*, is a nightmare in torture from beginning to end as we listen to the voices of those who have the job of turning an animal into food:

You can get frustrated when you're trying to move cattle along....sometimes, you have to prod them a lot. But some of the drivers like to burn the hell out of them. The five or six hotshots [electric prods] by the lead-up chutes are hooked directly to a 110 volt outlet. Run them along the floor's metal grates and they spit sparks like a welding machine. Some drivers would beat cattle with hotshots until they were so wild and panicky you couldn't do a thing

1 8

with them....A lot of times the skinner finds out an animal is still conscious when he slices the side of its head and it starts kicking wildly. If that happens, or if a cow is already kicking when it arrives at their station, the skinners shove a knife into the back of its head to cut its spinal cord.

Like the duck who tries to escape from the devouring flames, in the slaughterhouse hogs leap from the vats of scalding water they've been dumped into, while the skinners and knockers push them back in.

The literature from the Holocaust is vast and few can have escaped reading descriptions of the cattle cars the victims were carried in, the horrific beatings and starvation programs, the demonically modern form of death in the gas chambers. Always the screw is tightened by the inevitable sadist on hand:

All through that winter small children, stark naked and barefooted, had to stand out in the open for hours on end, awaiting their turn in the increasingly busy gas chambers. The soles of their feet froze and stuck to the icy ground. They stood and cried; some of them froze to death. In the meantime, Germans and Ukrainians walked up and down the ranks, beating and kicking the victims.
One of the Germans, a man named Sepp, was a vile and savage beast, who took special delight in torturing children. When he pushed women around and they begged him to stop because they had children with them, he would frequently snatch a child from the woman's arms and either tear the child in half or grab it by the legs, smash its head against a wall and throw the body away. (James Glass, *Life Unworthy of Life*, p. 122)

The attack upon the maternal instinct was carried to its height in Ravensbrück, the concentration camp set aside for women. If a woman had the misfortune to bear a child there, the infant was taken and drowned in a pail of water in front of her. It is said that often the mother and other women witnessing this, died on the spot. Germain Tillion called this death "anxiocution," or death from anxiety or horror.

The faculty of altruism is surely born in the maternal bond between mother and child, between the one whose body bears and the one being borne within the nourishing body. Nothing in nature is so ensuring that life means us well as the bond between mother and child, be it an animal mother and an animal offspring, duck and ducklings, cat and kittens, dog and pups, bear and cub; nothing so reassuring that there is a higher spirit in this world than our human selves as the sight of the animal who springs to the defense of her young at the cost of her own life.

To the researcher, however, pieties are impediments. A typical experiment to examine the birth process was conducted by the pediatrician, Dr. Raymond Stark, with a team of researchers. They made an incision into a monkey who was carrying a five month old fetus, perforated the uterus, took out the head of the fetus and made an incision into its head to expose its trachea and allow Dr. Stark to measure the fetus' breathing. He then inserted catheters into the carotid artery and jugular vein, and stitched the neck closed. Not finished, he twirled a drill bit into the fetus' forehead and inserted another catheter into the cerebral-spinal fluid, drilled three more holes into the top of the fetus' skull and inserted three more catheters, and still more catheters into the fetus' neck to measure the electrical activity of its heart. The fetus, looking like a pin cushion with six to eight protruding catheters from its body, was returned to the mother's uterus; incisions were closed except for the catheter tubes and wires from electrodes which were protruding from the mother's right side. The mother spent the next four weeks in a restraining chair to prevent her from pulling out the wires in her body. Then she died.

Dr. Stark made twelve such attempts for monkeys to deliver this way, and all failed. Dr. Stark explained: "The baboons like to give birth at night when no one is around. Because of the chair, and the catheters and electrodes, they can't properly tend to the infants with help, and they die." (Reported in the October issue of *Science* in 1984). The female baboon dies when she cannot help her child; the mother, witnessing her infant drowned in a pail of water, dies. The death instinct overwhelms when the maternal bond is broken; altruism is conquered by scientific narcissism.

Another experiment in the dynamics of mother love involved cauterizing the mammary glands of a rat who had just given birth to a litter. The baby rats could not suckle and died, while their mother ran around in frenzied circles. The ancient instinct had been cauterized for the sake of science.

What is the use of this experiment!

In Ethiopia a young mother, about eighteen but looking more like eighty, carries her famine-stricken baby fifty miles to a refuge center. Her teeth are yellow and large in her yellow gaunt face. She holds the baby to her dried out breasts which hang like empty bladders, like dried riverbeds, like a wadi under a bleached sun. Her eyes are ringed black with the misery of listening to her baby's last cries as it dies of starvation. Surely you've seen the pictures! If not from Ethiopia, then from the Sudan or elsewhere.

What is the use of experiments in mother love on rats and monkeys!

Harry Harlowe, the well-known researcher from the University of Wisconsin, whose work has been financed by taxpayer's dollars since 1967 to the tune of a million dollars a year, used to take newborn monkeys from their mothers and put them into a dark tunnel utterly deprived of light and sound, which he humorously called "the well of despair," to study the effects of sensory deprivation and separation of mother and child. Without such research, we might not know what afflicted the women of Ravensbrück when they saw an infant drowned in a pail of water. We might not know what happened to infants subjected to sensory deprivation and maternal separation. Luckily, there are photographs of the monkeys taken when they were retrieved from their "well of despair," so that we know. The photographs show a creature who has crawled into itself and looks like a mop with nothing to distinguish its head or tail or feet or eyes or mouth. Nothing left of its animal nature, it is a lump of unidentifiable fur except for two dead eyes that look like buttons. So now we know what happens when a creature is deprived of sensations and maternal nourishment.

Medical researchers, unlike slaughterers and butchers, claim that their work is necessary to advance medical progress, theirs is a "necessary evil," unlike eating meat which is only done for "the little taste upon the tongue." That is not the claim they always made. When the practice of vivisection arose as an academic discipline in the nineteenth century, vivisectors or physiologists as they were then called, argued that vivisection was done for philosophical reasons, for reasons to establish the scientific discipline of hardness, for reasons of asserting the eminence of materialism over the nasty moralistic habits of the past. Professor Léon Le Fort, at the Faculté de Médicine of Paris explained the purpose of vivisection thus:

> I do not mean to say that we claim for that method of investigation that it has been of any practical utility to medical science, or that we expect it to be so. But it is necessary as a protest on behalf of the independence of science against interference by clerics and moralists. When all the world has reached the high intellectual level of France, and no longer believes in God, the soul, moral responsibility or any nonsense of that kind, but makes practical utility the only rule of conduct,

then, and not till then, can science afford to dispense with vivisection.

The early nineteenth century French vivisector, François Magendie, boasted that he deliberately performed cruel experiments to destroy the "sentimental instincts" in himself. Claude Bernard, his disciple, boasted that he could perform ghastly experiments without feeling anything. Charles Richet, an eminent French physiologist in the nineteenth century, wrote:

> I do not believe that a single experimenter says to himself when he gives curare to a rabbit, or cuts the spinal cord of a dog, or poisons a frog, 'Here is an experiment that will relieve or cure the disease of some man.' No, in truth, he does not think that. He says to himself, 'I shall clear up some obscure point, I will seek out a new fact.' And this scientific curiosity which alone animates him is explained by the high idea he has formed of science. This is why we pass our days in foetid laboratories, surrounded by groaning creatures, in the midst of blood and suffering, bent over palpitating entrails.
> We find no hypercritical pretense here whether of utility or anesthetics, or of the comparative non-sensibility of the animals. The operator addresses himself to the public as frankly and as confident of their sympathy as we might conceive a devil addressing his fellow-devils to be, taking it for granted that the sentiments of humanity are as extinct in them as in himself.

Vivisectors were urged to transform themselves into human beings without feelings and took pride that they could, establishing emotional alienation as a modern value. Whatever improvements have been made in the conscience of animal

23

researchers is the result of thousands of hours of work on the part of animal rights protesters. The conscience of science itself, whether in the animal laboratory or elsewhere, is inert. It is not self-activating. It withered decades ago, diseased like a putrid appendix by its own philosophy of "value-free" science.

It is now pretty well conceded by medical historians and philosophers that lack of ethical concern in the medical profession is a crisis. Alfred Tauber quotes Alasdair MacIntyre: "...we have--very largely, if not entirely--lost our comprehension, both theoretical and practical, of morality." (*Confessions of A Medicine Man: An Essay In Popular Philosophy* p. 76). No surprise. That is how we train doctors.

Claude Bernard (1813-1878) is credited with being the father of physiology and of establishing not only the principles of animal experimentation but the necessary character of the vivisector. Unlike Magendie, Bernard was a writer (he had originally wanted to be a playwright and could use a pen): the animal researcher was a new type of human being who prided himself on having no moral center, who had extirpated ethical constraints and destroyed his instinct for pity. Bernard wrote:

> The physiologist is not an ordinary man: he is a scientist possessed and absorbed by the scientific idea that he pursues. He does not hear the cries of animals, he does not see their flowing blood, he sees nothing but his idea....

In himself, Bernard fused scientific objectivity and rationalism with the goals of a conscience-less science, one which would be unencumbered with the messy moral decisions other human beings are burdened with. He advised his disciple, Paul Bert, "...to leave his imagination outside on the coat rack with his coat before entering the laboratory." But he was aware of the dangerous potential in doing this and also advised him "not to forget to put it back on when he left the laboratory." Such a daring repression of moral sentiment should not be carried beyond the laboratory---but it was. In short time, unable to contain his zeal for experimenting, Bernard took home stray dogs and cut them open on the family kitchen table, eventually causing his wife to flee with her two daughters from their home. Unlike him, they could not shut their ears to the groans of the dogs.

He was a skillful surgeon with a particular interest in establishing the source of sugar in mammals. A typical experiment involved starving a nursing dog which still had milk in its mammary gland, injecting potassium prussiate into its jugular vein, killing it the next day and searching for prussiate and sugar in the blood serum. He often starved vegetarian animals such as rabbits to prove that they would consume the fat of their own bodies to stay alive, and declared that there is no "ultimate" vegetarian animal. He made many contributions to the study of the sugar chemistry of animals and was honored in his lifetime, being admitted to the prestigious Academy of Science in France. There are several statues of him on the campus of the Collège de Mèdicine in Paris. Knowledgeably, he commented on his career:

> If a comparison were required to express my idea of the science of life, I should say that it is a superb and dazzlingly, lighted hall which may be reached only by passing through a long and ghastly kitchen.

His book, *An Introduction to The Study of Experimental Medicine*, proved to be more influential than his actual discoveries. It asserted the primacy of the experimental method over observation and attempted to put medicine on the same footing as physics: i.e. to make medicine a deterministic science with predictable laws. Bernard had his doubts whether biology could be ultimately studied as inorganic matter, but he was determined to expunge the vitalistic principle from biology. When he first cut open a dog and looked into the "interior environment" of a living animal, he was astonished at the intricacy, design and organization:

It is as if there existed a pre-established design of each organism and of each organ such that...it reveals a special bond and seems directed by some invisible guide in the path which it follows and toward the position which it occupies. The simplest reflection reveals a primary quality, a *quid proprium* of the living being, in this pre-established organic harmony.

Elizabeth Blackwell, the first female doctor in the United States, experienced the same amazement, and it determined her to forsake vivisection. But Bernard rejected the implications of wonder and awe "pour la science."

> ....if the condition in which vital phenomena come to pass are infinitely many, complex and hard to grasp, assemble and master experimentally--they are nevertheless surely and fixedly linked to phenomena without any possibility of a *quid divinum* being invoked to explain them....

An admission of a *quid divinuum* would disturb his medical principle. "...vitalistic ideas...are just a kind of medical superstition--a belief in the supernatural....encourages ignorance and gives birth to a sort of unintentional quackery," he wrote. He had his doubts that biology would subscribe to immutable laws, but he understood that the experimental method, whatever its limitations, gave the experimenter great power:

> With the help of these active experimental sciences man becomes an inventor of phenomena, a real foreman of creation; and under this head we cannot set limits to the power that he may gain over nature through future progress in the experimental sciences.

By a marvelous compensation, science, in humbling our pride, proportionately increases our power. Men of science who carry experimental analysis to the point of relatively determining a phenomenon doubtless see clearly their own ignorance of the phenomenon in its primary cause; but they have become its master; the instrument at work is unknown, but they can use it. This is true of all experimental sciences in which we can reach only relative or partial truths and known phenomena only in their necessary conditions. But this knowledge is enough to broaden our power over nature.

He laid down the principle that power was more compelling than truth. The experimenter was "the foreman of creation." As his biographer, Reino Virtanen, said of him, "His physiology was...a fulfillment of Cartesian mechanism. It continues the current leading from the Beast-Machine through La Mettrie's Man-Machine...." (*Claude Bernard and His Place In The History of Ideas*, p. 29). After Bernard, the world closed conclusively on the sentient life of animals and was soon to close on the sentient life of humans. Eventually the view of the animal body as industrial waste leaked out of the laboratory.

It is a peculiarly modern phenomenon, this ability to reduce the individual to the non-being of an object and to completely cancel out moral discourse. How can one possibly engage in moral discourse with an object....? (James Glass, *Life Unworthy of Life*, p. 27)

From its inception in the mid nineteenth century until the present, animal research has been cruel. If we compare testimony given in "The British Parliamentary Investigation Into Vivisection Practises in 1875" and again with "The Second Royal Commission in 1906," and both with testimony given in "The United States Congressional Hearings Into Vivisection

27

Practices in 1962," we find no diminution of cruelty. Some might argue that, at least, anesthesia was used by the turn of the 20th century; but its use is often null, inadequately administered by research assistants or not used in experiments which require the animal to be conscious. Dr. Albert Leffingwell's book, *An Ethical Problem* (1916), is an early catalogue of ghoulish experiments that begins with the notorious French nineteenth century vivisector, J. Magendie. A description of one of his experiments was written up by Dr. Latour, "the founder and editor of the leading medical journal of France--*L'Union Médicale*" and which subsequently appeared in *The Lancet* and *The British Medical Journal* of August 22, 1863, so that the medical world was familiar with what was happening:

> I recall to mind a poor dog, the roots of whose vertebral nerves Magendie desired to lay bare to demonstrate Bell's theory, which he claimed as his own. The dog, already mutilated and bleeding, twice escaped from under the implacable knife, and threw his forepaws around Magendie's neck, licking, as if to soften his murderer and ask for mercy!

Often animals were subjected to further torments to make the research convenient for the researcher. Dr. Leffingwell describes a "scientific exploration" from the notebooks of Dr. L.J. Brachet, a famous nineteenth century doctor, recorded as Experiment 162:

> I inspired a dog with the strongest possible hatred for me by teasing it and inflicting upon it some pain every time I saw it. When this feeling had reached its height, so that the animal became furious when it saw or heard me, I put out its eyes. I could then appear before it without its manifesting any aversion. I spoke and immediately its barkings and furious

movements permitted no doubt of the rage which animated it.

I then destroyed the drum of the ears, and disorganized as much as I could of the inner ear. When the intense inflammation thus excited had rendered it almost deaf, I filled its ears with wax, and it could hear me no longer. Then I could stand by its side, speak to it in a loud voice, and even caress it, without awakening its anger....

Torturers could learn from this experimenter how to pacify a prisoner, and no doubt have, as we learned about mind control from Pavlov's experiments. Eventually it leaks out from the laboratory into the common world.

There were no restraints in what researchers felt they could do---as there were no restraints in what the SS felt they could do in the concentration camps. Elsewhere I have called the Nazi regime, "The Kingdom Without Limits," and so is the animal research laboratory:

> The means taken to depress the vital powers were as varied as the ingenuity of the vivisectors could devise. Sometimes it was accomplished by skinning the animal alive, a part of the body at a time, and then roughly 'sponging' the denuded surface. Sometimes it was secured by crushing the dog's paws, first one and then the other. Now and then the dog's feet were burnt, or the intestines exposed and roughly manipulated, the tail crushed, the limb amputated, the stomach cut out. Then came the 'stimulation' of the exposed nerve, carried on and repeated sometime until Nature refused longer to respond, and death came to the creature's relief. (Leffingwell, *An Ethical Problem,* p. 172-173)

This experiment was inflicted on a small eleven pound dog. His soul lives in me as do the souls of the children whose

2 9

feet froze to the ground on their way to the gas chamber. I feel their terrible confusion as death creeps into their toes. Every day, the disparity between innocence and human power, in children and in animals, afflicts me, and I welcome death for them who are beaten, electrocuted, burned, and skinned alive in the laboratories and the slaughterhouses. Death is the only friend innocence has in The Kingdom Without Limits.

The experimenter on the dog followed the path laid down by Charles Richet: he is totally unperturbed by any thought other than the experiment which, one notes with irony, was conducted for the purpose of understanding pain. In testimony given at the U.S. Congressional Hearing in 1962, there is the bizarre statement by a medical student that they do not anesthetize dogs because it is well known that dogs do not feel pain. (*The Dark Face of Science*, p. 189).

Pain is often not an issue in the curing process for doctors, though it is more often pain rather than the disease which demoralizes the patient. Loss of empathy in the medical profession is a substantive problem in disease management and "pain management," as it is called today, is a medical nightmare.

> Triumphant medicine could not have left us more alone, more ailing from the lack of a hand tapping that spot on the armchair where it rested forcefully so many times. We are left admiring its ticker-tape parades from behind iron bars of despair. (Ceronetti, *The Silence of The Body*, p. 228.)

There is a smoldering hiatus between the animal experiment and the reality of medical practice. The experimental method did not become the high road to enlightenment in medicine. Scientific barbarism teaches a subterranean lesson which lodges in the psyches of medical students like the subterranean places in which they practice their brutality. In *The Dark Face of*

30

Science, Vyvyan recorded some of the horrors which young medical students testified to at "The United States Congressional Hearings Into Vivisection Practices in 1962" (pp. 184-190).

> Trying to produce convulsions in dogs is terrible. I know they wouldn't let you see that, though. Shock experiments, removal of organs, blocking intestines, or the urine outlet so the bladder ruptures are only run of the mill...you'd be surprised to hear what professors and some students can think up." (p. 188)

> I am a student studying veterinary medicine. I was never and am not now in the employ of any humane society....This is a cry and a plea from a young person still holding on to a few ideals I have grown up to believe in--and I am beginning to wonder if there is any real human goodness among humans. I am not a sentimentalist, a crusader, or a fanatic; but I cannot, under my code of human life, condone what I, in a few short years have seen.(p. 187)

> I attended Chicago Medical School last September. I withdrew of my own accord....One of the conditions which led to my contempt towards this school was the cruel treatment which was given to the experimental animals. (p. 187)

Have we lost our best doctors who would have saved generations of cancer patients from the additional pain of medical indifference to their suffering?

Many of the experiments recorded by Dr. Leffingwell were conducted before the days of anesthesia, and many were public. Vivisection, or physiology, or biological research as it is now called, had not yet gone underground as it was to do at

3 1

the urging of Bernard who sensed that the public, unlike physiologists, had no stomach for this kind of medical practice.

When the British Parliament held its investigations into vivisection practices, the British public was aghast at what was revealed about these practices, but also aghast at the type of personality that such practice was breeding: One witness stated, "...From my experience...the glaring fault that was to be noticed was an entire want of feeling, that their feelings were entirely blunted; they seemed to be unconscious that they were inflicting the greatest pain...." (Westacott, *A Century of Vivisection and Anti-Vivisection,* p. 72) An apprehension overhangs the Parliamentary investigation that in the words of Frances Power Cobbe, there is coming "such a race of men" unknown before, something new in the makeup of humankind. John Graham, principle of Dalton Hall in Victoria University, Manchester, states: "This is a new incursion of reaction into human life. In the very highest part of human life, namely the intellectual side, the moral side is outraged...." (Ibid.). In his 1916 critique of vivisection, Dr. Leffingwell wrote, "...rarely, if ever, in the history of the world has a transformation of ideals, been more completely attained." (*An Ethical Problem.*) Medicine achieved a power that had been alien to itself, heretofore reserved for the dictator, the autocrat, the totalitarian emperor. A new type of intellectual had emerged.

As far as we know, Bernard was the first human being to deliberately split his personality between emotion and intellect, to deliberately practice emotional disaffection as a matter of principle, and he did it by practice on the animals. He gave rise to a new class of human being as decisively as Descartes' philosophy influenced the course of science. Robert J. Lifton identified this new human being as the" healer-killer" in *The Nazi Doctors*, and gave sociological resonance to the psychological phenomenon of "splitting." Robert Louis Stevenson had already dramatized the phenomenon in *Dr. Jekyll and Mr. Hyde* when he identified Dr. Jekyll as a physiologist.

"Why think when you can experiment?" Bernard said. In his biography on Mengele, Gerald Posner describes Mengele's insatiable appetite to experiment: "At such times it might seem that Mengele was motivated by sheer sadism, although most witnesses have remarked not at his pleasure at watching or inflicting suffering but at his total detachment from it." (p. 44) The puzzling reports of Mengele giving sweets to children before he experimented on them and playing games with them as he conducted them to the gas chamber cannot be understood in the context of sadism. The context is the cultivation of detachment which descended from Bernard's philosophy. "...the acts generated by autonomous technology occur in a kind of free fire zone, constrained only by the limitation of technical inventiveness." (Glass, p. 134) The excuse is that technology should not be judged---"it's what people do with technology."

It is often thought--and taught by those who have a stake in preaching this propaganda--that the Nazis did not experiment on animals because they experimented on people, though the evidence shows that animal experimentation led to, accompanied, and laid the legal foundation for human experimentation in Nazi Germany, as it does today. The evidence of Nazis experiments on animals is overwhelming. John Vyvyan in *The Dark Face of Science* summed it up correctly: "The experiments made on prisoners were many and diverse, but they had one thing in common: all were in continuation of, or complementary to experiments on animals. In every instance, this antecedent scientific literature is mentioned in the evidence: at Buchenwald and Auschwitz concentration camps, human and animal experiments were carried out simultaneously as parts of a single programme." (p. 159). These were the typhus experiments. Much of that "antecedent literature" is recorded in a book by Eugene Kogon, *The Theory and Practice of Hell* (1950), in the chapter, "Scientific Experiments." Kogon had been a political prisoner in Buchenwald where he served as a medical clerk in a laboratory where human experiments were conducted. His reports contain lists that include serum preparation made from rabbit lungs, mouse and rabbit livers, and typhus strains injected into guinea pigs. The notorious sterilization program carried out on concentration camp inmates was first developed on animals.

Once unleashed, freed from moral restraint, experimentation on animals and humans acquired a demonic drive because the metaphysics of modern life allows for, in fact requires the continual expansion of experimentation, including that of sentient creatures, until it squeezes out all other considerations.

So let us be done with comparisons between animal suffering and the Holocaust. Everyday is Treblinka for the animals, as Isaac Bashevis Singer said---Treblinka and Auschwitz. There are terrible cogent connections, dark connecting threads, between animal suffering and the Holocaust, but an embracing comparison between the two depletes both of meaning. If the argument was limited to barbarism and sentience there would be no argument; but the argument would be insufficient for both. The motives, causes and symbolism of each form of suffering differs vastly as it does with every form of suffering, and it is the task of the historian to trace the motives, causes and symbolism of suffering when they are embedded in the laws, institutions, and social habits of a society. Unless we do this, each victim, human or animal, Jew or non-Jew, becomes a generalized metaphor for any other victim, and understanding of the how and the why of cruel institutions such as slavery or war or concentration camps is obliterated. History is obliterated in a wash of metaphors.

On the level of sentience, the concentration camp victim, the slave in chains bound and whipped, the animal skinned for its fur or its food, should share the ground of common visceral revulsion. "Pain is Pain no matter who suffers it." There is no proof that the flesh of a burning human being is hotter than the flesh of a burning animal. We may think so because the human race has left a record of its suffering, and the animals have not. They have lived their pain in secret places, with little trace on human consciousness. The human gifts of language and writing--in short, of history--have brought for us greater attention and consciousness of our suffering; they have added dignity to our suffering, while animal suffering is barely accorded knowledge. It is history which separates animal suffering from the Holocaust.

The Holocaust is largely the result of the convergence of three historical streams: the history of Germany after the First World War with the imposition of the Versailles treaty on Germany; the history of anti-Semitism and its prismatic focal intensity in Hitler; and the history of science and technology from the mid-nineteenth century. This latter history includes such Enlightenment principles as rationalism as the centralizing human principle, and the use of science to promote racist ideas, which converged with historical anti-Semitism. Aside from metaphysical or religious interpretations of the causes of the Holocaust (not to be confused with metaphysical or religious interpretations of the *consequences* of the Holocaust) the Holocaust was largely the result of this troika of forces, each of which have been studied and analyzed in a myriad number of books, and each of which exists in the realms of history and sociology and can be traced in books, documents, speeches, or whatever else historians use to compile and understand history.

The human abuse of animals lies outside this history. Its roots are in an older relationship between the human race and the animal world, a relationship which antedates any intelligible record we have of their relationship which is, as the art historian Kenneth Clarke observed, strangely paradoxical, made up of equal parts of reverence, affection, idolatry, need, contempt, and cruelty, exhibiting in strongest outline Oscar Wilde's famous aphorism: "Each man kills the thing he loves." Ted Kerasote's book, *Bloodties: Nature, Culture and the Hunt,* examines the relationship between the "true" hunter and the animal he kills, beginning with a quotation from Elgin Gates, the famous trophy hunter:

> The true trophy hunter is a self-disciplined perfectionist seeking a single animal, the ancient patriarch well past his prime that is often an outcast from his own kind. This hunter is a mixture of sportsman and conservationist, testing his skills and resources against the crafty instincts and wariness of a wise old ram, hunting with the intent to kill the very animal he admires.

This hunter has contempt for those whose only aim is to kill an animal. Kerasote quotes Bob Kubick, another famous trophy hunter:

> The old-timers hunted sheep because they loved sheep, because they loved to be up on those high windswept ridges where they shared the sheep pastures with the sheep, the grizzly, the hoary marmot, the soaring eagle. When they brought back a ram trophy, they were not seeking honor and prestige--they were bringing back memories of icy winds fragrant with fir and balsam, of the smell of sheep beds and arctic willow, of tiny perfect alpine flowers, gray slide rock, velvet sheep pastures. The old-timers had sheep and sheep country in their blood.

The passage almost suggests that past ages are encoded in our brains, alive in the hunter's brain. Other passages in Kerasote's book speak of the sad dependency and guilt humans have felt towards animals. This from an Abnaki hunter: "I have killed you because I need your skin for my coat and your flesh for my food. I have nothing else to live on."

Such emotions, needs, and impulses are antithetical to those the Nazi brought to the Jews he killed. We will never understand the hunter or the Nazi by standards of comparisons and associations, for each developed out of different traditions within different historical matrices, and for different reasons. Of all human emotions, hatred is the simplest, the deadliest perhaps but also the simplest, tolerating no leaven of ambiguity or contradiction. Love and affection must often put up with guilt, remorse, exhaustion, impatience, and jealousy, but pure hatred is exactly that, while there is no such thing as pure love.

Animal suffering and hatred for the Jew come closest in the industrial complex where animals are reduced to machines. Contempt and abuse are the inevitable consequences of those in power over the powerless in this setting. "Life unworthy of life" and life deemed useful for life elicit similar responses in the bleak utilitarianism of the industrial world. Human suffering in the modern world is now symbolized by the concentration camp, the bleakest form of utilitarianism, where human beings were rendered into industrial waste. The format of breeding and death is common for both animal and human, regarded as an efficient, rationalized system for producing food or reducing humans to death. Several strands in the causes of the Holocaust overlap with these specific modern forms of cruelty towards animals, and even with the metaphysical posture of the Nazis in their pursuit of biological purity. Gerald Posner, in his biography of Mengele, says of him that "He believed you could create a new super-race as though you were breeding horses." Himmler learned a similar lesson in his pre-Nazis profession as a chicken farmer. The eighteenth century expanded the idea of breeding through practice on animals, (Harriet Ritvo, *The Animal Estate*) and soon analogies between animals and humans took place on a new plane, augmented by the scientific view of breeding. Simply put, the Nazi question was: why couldn't you breed a human being as you breed an animal? For this purpose, land must be put aside, enough land to house thousands.

And first there is the land on which feed lots, battery hen cages, and human concentration camps are created:

> Most outdoor feedlots are a series of small, flat, fenced fields each holding a hundred or so animals. Individual capacity varies enormously, but feedlots of over a hundred thousand head are common, with the animals crowded on the treeless, flyblown, dusty lots stretching out to the horizon....The analogy [to human concentration camps] is plain and undeniable; for both groups are held at the mercy of unfeeling keepers, deprived of freedom, crowded into small spaces, mutilated, tattooed, branded, and permanently marked, subjected to genetic experimentation--and ultimately murdered." (C. David Coats, *Old MacDonald's Factory Farm,* p. 72-78)

Rabbi Everett Gendler describes his surprise and dismay when he and his wife came across a structure which looked like a factory, but was a multi-storied huge concrete building housing thousands and thousands of birds confined to cages the size of a newspaper. "...there were no signs of other habitations around, no sizable towns on the map....Often there is only a dirt road leading to these structures. The land around is usually dead, arid, waste, brown. The long buildings give no hint of the seething torment inside anymore than the wall around a prison does." (Roberta Kalechofsky,*Vegetarian Judaism*, p. 121.)

So too the German concentration camps were usually founded on "dead" land that was not useful for anything else. Like factory farming, it was a business whose ultimate goal was to wring every conceivable profit from creatures. Germaine Tillion was an anthropologist imprisoned in Ravensbrück, the only concentration camp for women, because she had been a member of the French Resistance. She used her professional training to leave a record of concentration camp life in her book, *Ravensbrück.* The camp was "a center for the economic exploitation of female prisoners--it was a profit making industrial enterprise which waited until the last minute to 'settle' its labor costs and liquidate its 'manpower.'" (p. 39) The camp had been founded by Himmler, in addition to six others by him: Mauthausen, Dachau, Treblinka, Bergen-Belsen, Sachsenhausen and Auschwitz, from which Himmler received revenues as his personal property. Goering received a fourth of the profits from Buchenwald. Stock in the camps was sold and dividends were paid. The concentration camp--as well as the slave camp in the Gulag--was "A perfect utilization of uncultivated wasteland for an ingenious capitalist: where nothing grows, a concentration camp is built...." (Ibid., p. 46.) A few hundred years after Jews ceased to be expelled from European countries for usury, this Christian greed claimed its pound and more of Jewish flesh. This was a business--like factory farming --but with exceptions, crucial to the human situation. Prisoners were beaten for misbehaving, and they were used for slave labor. The women in Ravensbrück supplied the labor for fifty-five industries--as well as the sex and entertainment for the Nazi officers.

We do not know whether masturbating animals in the laboratories to harness their sperm is experienced as "sexual entertainment," as a "turn-on" or a "put down." But what of the animal being masturbated time and again under anesthesia? The means nature devised for her fecundity is manipulated by the gloved fingers of a researcher to wrench some semen for an experiment.

The Jew was not treated like an animal, nor is the animal treated like the Jew. To the Nazi mind, the Jew was treated like a Jew, an anomaly, a mistake, a disease, a contamination, something that could bring disaster to the German people and then to the human race if he were not exterminated, something whose semen was feared as contamination and to be sterilized, irradiated, not harvested and preserved. No such ideas pertain to animals. Pain and cruelty visited upon them is for wholly different reasons. Some may argue that, given the horrific suffering of both, this is a petty distinction, and with respect to sentience it is, but to the Jew, to the history of anti-Semitism, to the necessary understanding of the why and wherefore of the Holocaust, it is anything but petty. Without the history of anti-Semitism, the Holocaust would never have happened. The Second World War would probably have happened---but not the Holocaust. They have separate histories arising out of separate weltanschauungs, regardless of how they have become braided together in the popular understanding. For the Jew, it is important that they not be entwined, because everyday the Jew inherits the legacy of anti-Semitism, whether Hitler would have happened or not.

The tentacles of the Holocaust reach back through two millennia, but much of its pertinent shape took place in the 12th century, the century which has been called "the Medieval Renaissance." In *Order and Exclusion*, Dominique Iogna-Pratt traces the transformation of anti-Judaism into anti-Semitism and the emergence of the racial definition of "the Jew." By the early 1300's a question was being posed to children in school texts, concerning the differences between Jews and Christians: "The question hinged on whether Jewish men were subject to periodic bleeding like the menstrual flows of women. The answer given was affirmative." (p. 321) Peter the Venerable, ninth abbot of Cluny already contemplated the idea of the extermination of the Jews, and decided on the famous Christian "final solution," that the Jews were to be kept alive to be converted as witnesses to the truth of Jesus Christ. Iogna-Pratt reflects on Peter the Venerable's problem:

> Dealing with the Jewish question meant, for Christians, ridding themselves of an alter ego, breaking from the

constraints of the intellectual Semitism at the root of Christianity. The way out of the Christian identity crisis lay in reducing the Jew to detritus of history, relegating them outside time to the role of witnesses. Fixing them in the past as the theological counterpart of a process of social isolation. (p. 361)

How can the historian from the age of the Shoah not be alarmed in retrospect when he sees the Abbot of Cluny railing against the Jews as the murderers of Christ and wondering if they really belong to the human race.
(p. 276)

The road to the Holocaust has been well documented by now in countless studies of anti-Semitism by both Jews and Christians.(Most recently, *Constantine's Sword*, by James Carroll; earlier, *The Conflict Between Church and Synagogue* by James Parkes, *The Crucifixion of the Jews* by Father Flannery, *The Teaching of Contempt* by Jules Isaac, *Towards A Definition of Anti-Semitism* by Gavin Langmuir.) From its rise in the 4th century when Christianity was declared the state religion of the Roman empire to the 20th century, Jews have lived in Christian lands under the opprobrium of the deicide charge, of being "Christ-killers." Their lives and their history have been shanghaied by Christianity, their destiny sewn into the fabric of another people, their character judged as "a deicide people," as "perfidious," according to Christian theology. There is no relationship in the world like the relationship between Christian and Jew, where an entire nation, a culture, a civilization, has become embedded into the theology, the myths, the fables, the eschatology, of another people without hope of release. Jews are hostage to the Christian religion. They stand under the charge of "the accursed and the accused," a charge that may lessen at different times and in different places, but is always a substratum of Christian thought, dignified by scriptural authority:

> "When the chief priests therefore and officers saw him, they cried out, saying, Crucify *him*, crucify *him*. Pilate saith unto them, Take ye him, and crucify him; for I find no fault in him...they cried out, Away with *him*, away with him, crucify *him*...." (John, 19: 6-15. King James Version)

The mark of fiction is on the writing, for what legitimate court holds a trial at predawn "before the cock crows?" Still it is enshrined as a dramatic event, as history in the Easter liturgy, and as history in a thousand years of art, passion plays, poems, folk literature, and songs:

> Were you there when they crucified my Lord?

Ruth Mellinkof's amazing analysis of medieval art, *Outcasts*, demonstrates how art enforces propaganda. The Jew and the Infidel were usually painted in particular colors, the Jew usually in yellow. Even where there was no language, the public knew at a glance who the enemy of Christ was. He is mnemonically available in song and art in the view of the Jew as the deicide Jew, the accursed Jew, the accused Jew, the wandering Jew, the cunning Jew, the greedy Jew, the carnal Jew, the clever Jew, the twisted Jew, the crooked Jew, the perfidious Jew, the two-faced Jew, the usurious Jew, the cosmopolitan Jew, the tribal Jew, the communist Jew, the capitalist Jew, the stiffnecked Jew, the New York Jew, the legalistic Jew salivating for his pound of flesh, the eye for an eye Jew whose God is a storm god, a thunder god, a god of power and vengeance, while the Christian practises the mercy that falls from the heavens above because his god is a god of love and forgiveness.

Who wouldn't want to be a Christian and have such a nice god? According to Christian theology, the Jews especially should want to be Christian, since Christ came to save them. Why they don't baffles many Christians. Why would anyone think well of Jews who turn down the offer of eternal life, who do not accept such a nice god as Jesus Christ and his sacrifice? Hence, classic Christianity teaches that the Jews must be a perfidious people to reject Christ. In the Manichean world represented by two halves of one Bible, popularly called "the Old" and "the New," split between a god of thunder, vengeance, and the material world and a god of forgiveness and love, the Jew symbolizes opposite qualities, he symbolizes whatever is the social irritation, communism or capitalism. He is the irritation. If the Jew stands for THE LAW, he provokes the thrill of lawlessness in the anti-Semite scrawling a swastika on a synagogue door, or digging up a Jewish grave and urinating into it. Often there is a potent sexuality to Jew hatred, a form of deophiliac.

In *Voyage of Discovery,* James Parkes records his first face to face encounter with anti-Semitism, when he chaired a Christian student conference in Switzerland in 1925, on the subject of "The Jewish Question," to which one lone Jewish Rumanian student had been invited to state the case for the Jews. Parkes recorded that "The response of his Christian opponent was so venomous" that the event determined Parkes' career to explain such furious Christian hatred for the Jew. As Gavin Langmuir observes in *Toward A Definition of Antisemitism,* what is unusual about anti-Semitism is its "chimerical character." (p. 17) The Jew as the enemy of Christ becomes the enemy of everything good.

In Celine's writing anti-Semitism is carried to orgiastic irrationality.

> He's mimetic, he's a whore, he would have dissolved long ago, after assimilating to others so much, if it weren't for his greed, his greed saves him, he has worn

out all races, all men, all animals, the earth is now done with....He's still hassling the universe, heaven, God, the Stars, he wants everything, he wants more, he wants the Moon, he wants our bones, he wants our guts as hair-curlers to celebrate the Sabbath, to deck the Carnival. (Julia Kristeva, *Powers of Horror: An Essay on Abjection*, p. 181.)

The Jew inspires a dizzying phantasmagoria of symbols, symbols crushed on top of symbols, symbols obliterating and melting into other symbols. No other creatures, human or non-human, carry such symbolic overload. Rarely does an animal arouse such sexualized paroxysms of hatred from its killer. Only in the pageantry of the bullfight does killing an animal carry an erotic discharge. To the trapper who traps and skins a beaver, the beaver is a beaver. Other emotions would be regarded as mad. The trapper traps and skins the beaver precisely because it is a beaver. To the anti-Semite, the Jew is always something else, the bearer of a universal stigmata the anti-Semite feels in his flesh, the messenger from a god he fears. The beaver is killed because his fur or his meat is useful. The usefulness of the Jew's body in the death camps--the recycled hair, the gold teeth pulled from his mouth, the soap made from his body fat--was incidental. Jews were not destroyed for their usefulness, but for opposite reasons. They were destroyed under the motto of "life unworthy of life." This is not the argument used against animals. No one thinks of the beaver, the mink, the leopard, the elephant as "life unworthy of life."

Alfred Rosenberg, head of Hitler's foreign policy department, gave the definitive reason for Jew hatred in his article, "The Earth-Centered Jew lacks A Soul":

> The world is preserved...only by a positive yea-saying to the world. Among the Jewish people this world-affirmation is totally pure, without any

admixture of world-denial. All other nations that have ever existed, and exist today, had, or have, such an admixture characterized by the idea of a Hereafter.... (quoted in George Mosse, *Nazi Culture*, p. 75)

Denis de Rougement states in *Passion and Society*, "Every doctrine of immortality implies a tragic preoccupation with death." He believes that Christianity never shook itself free of its Marcion and Manichean influence and that its passion is historically for death, to release the soul from its material degradation; its love of heroism and war is a search for the means to dissolve consciousness and the unadventurous quotidian in the intoxication of death. Of course, ordinary people do not think this way. Ordinary people cling to life with more or less intensity and soldiers try not to get killed in war. But the hero's death is a recurrent theme, however filled with nostalgic pathos, and the views of philosophers, writers and theologians work a leaven in every society.

Next to "the usurious Jew," the favorite epithet for Jews in the Middle Ages was "the carnal Jew," not because Jews were sexier than Christians, but because they were observed to be earthbound embracers of the world. True. Judaism, in its essence, opposes longing for death and the eroticization of death. Wagner's music is the apotheosis of death-longing. Jacques Barzun says of Tristan, "...sensation is for the sake of forgetting self, love is for the sake of death....Nowhere is anyone found saying 'yea' to life, loving his fate, knowing his mind or shaping the world. It is the Bayreuthian era of civilization." (*Darwin, Marx, and Wagner*, p. 302) Wagner's personality structure was similar to Hitler's. Both felt destined, and did not care a hoot what form their destiny took as long as their egos could be writ large in it, both had the ability to enslave people, friends, worshippers, mobs, audiences. Both were narcissistic, destructive, and cared nothing for those who befriended and helped them. Both worshipped art beyond humans and used art for inflammatory purposes. Their egos

4 5

gnawed at them to devise means to express destruction writ large in music or war. They worshipped death under the guise of nobility and epitomized de Rougement's statement, "Death is the ideal goal of lofty men."

To the Christian, the Jewish God is a god of vengeance, vindictiveness, a thunder-God, "the eye-for-an-eye" god. To Jews, their God is a God Who delights in life. The messenger from The Kingdom of Death, Alfred Rosenberg, understood this. For him it was cause to exterminate the Jews, as one who relishes the taste of death would exterminate the breath of life in his mouth.

The Holocaust is the descendant of the relationship between Christian and Jew, a relationship that has no metaphoric extension to any other relationship, and seems impossible to extirpate. "Already by the end of the thirteenth century many Christians in northern Europe were manifesting the same kind of irrational hostility toward Jews that Hitler would express." (Langmuir, p. 15) There are many extraordinarily good-willed Christians who are working to break the dark thread of Christian-Jewish relations, but the forces of opposition are very strong. "The stubborn survival of symbols and signs, once firmly planted and nourished in a culture, never ceases to amaze." (Mellinkoff, p.48). One would have to obliterate much of Christian religious art, much literature, Chaucer, The Merchant of Venice, Pound, Eliot, Wyndham Lewis, thousands of songs, ditties, jokes, passion plays, Wagner, in short, European culture, even saints like Chrysostom. He was a vegetarian and we would have had a lot in common. Too bad he was such an anti-Semitic wonk. Voltaire said that the claims of the brutes to rights went back to the Bible. "The Lord makes covenants with the beasts of the field. He does not make them with rocks." It's one of my favorite quotes. Too bad that on a visit to a ghetto Voltaire called the Jews who lived there "vermin." His repugnance gives one an idea of the horrific conditions of an eighteenth century ghetto, and Voltaire didn't care to inquire further. He also owned stock in a slave ship. So much for enlightenment!

Once one gets on to history's (s)hit list, it's hard to get off. Christian and Nazi anti-Semitism have made a triumphal entry into the Islamic world, which gorges its appetite on such books as *The Protocols of the Elders of Zion,* while the United States and Europe finance the purveyors of this hate literature that is outlawed in many of their own countries. It is too early to tell how European anti-Semitism will work its way into Islamic religious symbolism. At the moment, Islamic anti-Semitism is political, with efforts to build on the deicide charge by telling Muslims that the Jews killed the prophet Jesus. Islam is forbidden by its religion to speak of Jesus as a god or as the son of god, and while "prophet-killer" carries a charge it's not the deadly ring of deicide. The trenchant Islamic religious issue is that Jews trespassed the Islamic religious code by breaking free of their minority or "dhimmi" status that Jewish communities had in the Islamic world, and that they established a state for themselves. Many Christians have trouble with this too, for both Christianity and Islam are supercessionist religions.

Christianity is making an effort to shake its supercessionist relationship with Judaism, but in its historical panoply the relationship between Christians and Jews is unique, and nothing like it exists between humans and animals or foetuses. Even when Hitler lost his attachment to Christianity, he saw himself as the avenging angel of its history. With respect to the Jew, his mission was utterly religious and not political and that is why he did not hesitate to sacrifice German soldiers and war necessities to his goal of destroying the Jew. That is why his last message to the German people written in his coffin-bunker was to finish the war against the Jews.

Christianity did not preach the death of the Jew. The official Christian teaching is that the Jew is to be kept alive as a witness and converted. But that message bred contempt for the

Jew as Jew, and Hitler was not alone in converting that message into death. The first really tough era for the European Jew came with the first crusades beginning in 1095, when the crusaders poured out of Europe, down from the north across France and into Italy, killing every Jew they could find in their wake. How ironic that Islamic propaganda includes Jews in its "anti-crusader" message when the Jews were the first victims of the Crusades and died together with the Muslims in Jerusalem when the Crusaders stormed that city. (Such is the protean nature of anti-Semitism.) The era of Jewish massacres had started, followed by mini massacres and then large ones in the 14th century when Jews were accused of spreading the bubonic plague, which resulted in over four hundred massacres of Jews. Sixty very large communities and one hundred and fifty small communities were eliminated. The massacres were followed by five hundred years in the ghettoes under conditions of such filth, Voltaire held his nose when he passed through one. Ghetto life was accompanied and followed by pogroms, until finally the Jews were released into the modern world by Napoleonic decree, followed by a century of civic laws and gentlemen's agreements that barred them from universities and public office. The emancipation of the Jew was not completed in Germany until 1918. Emancipated, he flung himself into the modern world with five hundred years of pentup energy and talent, but his successes in the arts, in medicine, in science, in music was tallied up against him. As Kafka remarked, "The European intellectual forgives the Jew nothing." His appearance in German cities and towns as a "free person" was noted with hostility. Germany, as other European countries, was going through a revulsion against city life as the locus of modern industrial depravity. The terms, "rootless," and "cosmopolite," for Jew were contextually deadly. The development of the "volk" mystique, rooted in Wagner's medievalism, excluded the Jew who had been landless in the medieval economy. Hitler had his ear to the ground and understood both the modern meaning of "Jew" and the two millennia of accusations against the "perfidious" Jew: the Jew was an anomaly in the modern world as he had been an anomaly in the mystic past of the "volk"; he was a pollution that had to be eliminated--not merely killed, but eliminated so that there would be no trace of his existence, nothing that could ever again be recognized as "Jew." Death was insufficient, because that which is a pollution cannot be merely buried in the ground because it will pollute the earth. It must be pulverized until there is no identifying mark left. Not even half-identity must be left to that which is conceived of as "dirt" or "rubbish" or "pollution."

In *Purity and Danger,* Mary Douglas analyzes the ritual processes undertaken by tribes to extirpate that which they perceive as "the anomalous," that which cannot be assimilated into their cosmology or religion. There is "...a long process of pulverizing, dissolving, and rotting away of any physical things that have been recognized as dirt. In the end, all identity is gone. The origin of the various bits and pieces is lost and they have entered into the mass of common rubbish." (p. 160) "Where there is no differentiation there is no defilement." (Ibid.) Thus, the garbage heaps of bodies in the camps, the common graves that lack identification, the reduction of bodies to ashes.

Proper burial is one of the things that defines a human being. Antigone accepts death in order to bury her brothers and prevent Creon from reducing them to carrion. It is an urge so profound among humans that soldiers run out into enemy fire to bring back their dead for burial. A body buried as waste invokes our deepest dread of meaninglessness.

In the middle ages, the bodies of heretics were dug up and burned. Death was not enough. Pollution must be fought with fire and ashes. The identity of the contaminant must be erased, burned with fire, reduced to ashes. The crematorium found its symbolic fulfillment.

The author of an anonymous diary found in Auschwitz wrote, "'We're not human beings anymore, nor have we become animals; we are just some strange psycho-physical product 'made in Germany.'" (Glass, p. 27, quoting from Harold Kaplan, *Conscience and Memory,* p. 130).

The word most often associated with the camps is "uncanny." "Disconcerted logic," is what Julia Kristeva calls "uncanniness" and identifies it with loss of self (*Strangers To Ourselves*, p. 187). The "container" of the personality dissolves; the human being experiences himself as "indistinct," without boundaries, without even memories of a self. Uncanniness "is a destruction of the self." James Glass says the Jew in the camps was regarded as "industrial waste," "useless biological matter." (p. 35-36). "Groups seen to be impure found themselves encircled in a medical language filled with images of pollution and infection," (p. 35) as the Jew had been encircled by a Christological language for almost two thousand years. The final attack was not on the body alone, but through the body on the Jew as an anomaly that had to be reduced to a rubbish heap. Yes, there was something new under the sun, something different from historic torture and historic assaults of revenge on enemies, something different from the avenging sword of the crusader and the lynch mob, something which Hitler had picked up in the rubble of anti-Semitic thought and merged with the German desire for racial purity. "Science in the Third Reich sanitized paranoia, disguising hatred of the Jew in the language and practice of a biological-medical argument premised on identifying the Jew with infection." (Glass, p.127) Glass' analysis of the "Auschwitz mentality," takes it place in the history of the animal research laboratory mentality, bred by François Magendie and Claude Bernard, the nineteenth century "fathers' of animal research, and taught for generations to medical researchers as "guiltless biological morality." (Glass, p. 129) The "Auschwitz mentality" was the imposition of the animal research mentality on historic anti-Semitism, but it was historic anti-Semitism that bubbled up out of the unconscious where it resides in fantasy, images and symbols different from those of the hunter's, the trapper's or the bullfighter's.

No such fantasies, images or symbols as those used to brand the Jew attach themselves to the animals. Except under unusual conditions of plague or endemic disease, animals are not considered public health menaces. Though he has learned how to pulverize the animal's body into waste, the animal researcher does not symbolize or allegorize the animal he makes sick, Neither does the butcher carry on a symbolic war with the animal he carves up, though those who are carnivores have plenty of symbolic associations with eating meat as do those who wear fur. Greed, vanity, scientific careerism, commercialism---there are plenty of reasons why human beings are cruel to animals, but all the reasons are summed up by the fact of human power over the vulnerable. That human power reached its zenith in the modern world in the laboratory where human beings were taught to overstep all boundaries, where they learned how to inflict learned helplessness on animals, lessons concentration camp guards found useful. Reduced to biological confusion, to a state where the victim does not experience his body, the victim became confused about his own survival, often would not eat, often would not wash; excretory functions came and went in whatever fashion. In *The Survivor*, Terrence Des Pres notes that the first step on the way to biological death of the concentration camp victim was alienation from the body.

Nakedness was important to producing this alienation and "learned helplessness" in human beings. Nakedness was not only used to produce discomfort, cold, shame, but to rob the victim of past associations of status, class, religion, social context, individuality in choice of color or the rag of a ribbon that suggested an esthetic. The human being was robbed of associations and context, of his Jewishness, then the body was reduced to industrial waste and, in the interests of efficiency, recycled out as animal fat to be used for other products.

5 1

Excrement was also important in the process. Excrement was not an accidental product as it is in the animal laboratories and in the battery hen cages, but neither is comparison with the battery hen cages out of place, for excremental buildup is inimical in the industrial processing of both chickens and human death: As Karen Davis writes in *Prisoned Chickens, Poisoned Eggs,* "Manure is everywhere in the caged layer complex. Toxic ammonia rises from the decomposing uric acid in the manure pits beneath the cages to produce a painful corneal condition in chickens known as 'ammonia burn'....the manure fumes and rotting carcasses force workers in the houses to wear gas masks...." In the concentration camp, excrement was *intended* as part of the killing process of reducing and wasting. It was part of what Terrence des Pres has called "excremental assault." In Auschwitz there was one toilet, a large hole in the ground for thirty thousand prisoners, and no toilet paper. Prisoners had to wipe themselves with their own clothes and wear those clothes. They were often forced to eat their food out of their unwashed slop buckets. Many were forced to urinate into the mouths of others. Dysentery was common and prisoners relieved themselves standing on their feet or lying in their beds. Their bodies rotted in their own ordure, they rotted standing on line, they rotted lying in their beds. They could smell themselves rotting. "In the most bizarre cases, defilement caused a desperation bordering on madness." Defilement, Paul Ricoeur, states in De Pres' book, is "'the oldest of the symbols of evil,'" chosen for the Jew from the logic of Nazi anti-Semitism . No such strategy is used in hunting, skinning, slaughtering or experimenting on animals. Degradation is useless in the hunter's or the trapper's assault, but was sought as a strategy for the human, specifically for the Jewish human, marking a division between human and animal.

Humiliation and shame were strategically implemented in the concentration camps. Human values were stripped away to destroy human identity. Decrees "against individual identity" had been passed earlier. All male Jews were to be called Abraham, all female Jews were to be called Sarah. All Jews were declared to be the same Jew. Nakedness and excrement-- forced reversion to infantilism--these were tools in the process of the deconstruction of identity and personhood.

> The unacknowledged body ceases to possess human qualities and therefore exists outside of any moral universe of care. The body possesses no meaning; it is perceptually transformed into waste; it may be broken up into parts of 'scientific' experimentation. (Glass, p. 25)

Standard procedure in animal research laboratories. Animals are inoculated with bacilli, made sick, then killed, then their tissues are pulverized in machines that look like kitchen blenders, to be made into slides to be studied. Nakedness is not a technique useful to the animal researcher. Excremental buildup in animal cages is not a deliberate part of the killing process. It is caused by the inevitable disregard for creatures who won't be able to snitch on you, who depend for a clean cage on the semi-annual visit of an inspector. The most useful technique the animal researcher learns is the deconstruction of his conscience, of superego constraints, as Glass describes the Nazis doctors: "Superego or conscience had been destroyed through an alliance of scientific objectivity, bureaucratic functionalism, and the moral blindness of technology."

Animals, like the Jew in the mind of the Christian, are often a symbol of unconscious and repressed fears, in addition to the affection and reverence they inspire. To the Christian the deicide charge reflects the Jews' denial of Christ's claim as the Messiah and/or son of God, or reflects the Christian's fears about Christ's claim or his loathing of monotheism. Many Nazis were anti-Catholic because they viewed Catholicism as the heir to Judaism. Alfred Rosenberg loathed Jesus because he did not represent Nordic courage, and loathed Judaism because "Jesus was a Jew." To the Christian, the Jew is guilty for killing Jesus; to the Nazi he was guilty for creating him. Again, the reasons are chimerical and endless. One can access "anti-Semitism" on the internet and find a cornucopia of explanations for Christian or Nazi or Islamic anti-Semitism.

The symbolic value of the animal varies in different cultures. The Greeks, keen on rationality, at least so far as their conscious lip service suggests, defined the animal as "irrational," and feared it for that reason. E. R. Dodds reflects their fear in *The Greeks and The Irrational*, a book which tells us more about the Greeks than the ad nauseam analyses of Socrates' death. Classical Buddhism, while it teaches non-injury to animals, also teaches that animals occupy the lowest rung of animate life along with hell beings and hungry ghosts. Even in religions that teach reincarnation, animals often occupy an unenviable place in the cosmology. Even in religions that believed that some animals were gods or goddesses, or had power over human destinies, animals were sacrificed, eaten, and hunted. The variety of rationalizations practised by human beings in their pursuit of animal food, clothing, and animal labor, would be amusing in another context. The Greeks would put bells and ribbons on a sacrificial cow and manipulate its head up and down to signify that the animal consented to his slaughter. The Hindus believe that "the sacrifice of an animal *is not really the killing of an animal.*" (Italics author) (Basant K. Lal, "Hindu Perspectives on the Use of Animals in Science") A sad irreconciliation pervades this belief, for the Hindu, like others who practised animal sacrifice, recognizes the suffering of the animal and wishes to wish it away:

> The animal to be sacrificed is not considered an animal; it is, instead, a *symbol*, a symbol of those powers for which the sacrificial ritual stands....What is important for sacrificial ritual is not the object to be offered in sacrifice but

following the elaborate rites and scrupulously observing the traditional rules.

Like the Jew, the animal has become trapped into the religion and symbolism of another group. The animal's life and destiny are under the control of the symbolic signs of others. He, of course, does not suffer as a symbol; he suffers and dies as an animal, but the Jew suffers and dies as a symbol in addition to his biological death. The Holocaust lives in an historic and symbolic context different from that of animals, even though analogues of their suffering could fill catalogues, and even though one of the bridges that led to the Holocaust was the reduction of the laboratory animal to a non-sentient object, "a peculiarly modern phenomenon," as Glass calls it. Eventually the method and philosophy creep out of the laboratory, and the dark side of human nature finds expression in the dark face of science.

Two questions are often asked about the Holocaust: 1)Haven't we had enough books on the subject? No, because the union of science, fascism, and totalitarianism is a new phenomenon and we need to know everything about it; 2) Is the Holocaust unique? This question casts a long shadow over modern life, informing us of what a nation looks like when value-free scientific agendas and paradigms rule over old ideas, old symbols, old atavisms, old hostilities. "'Hitler came to power because he made it possible for German citizens to think of their dreams of destruction as a science with a biological basis.'" (Glass, p. 113) So powerful are scientific and medical arguments in the modern world that death, destruction, and torture can be justified in the name of science, knowledge, and progress. James Carroll has called the Holocaust "revelatory." So it is. It is revelatory of Christian and European history, revelatory of every decree passed against Jews for seventeen hundred years, revelatory of every Jew street than runs through European cities and towns, revelatory of five hundred years of ghetto life. That is why animal suffering cannot be compared to it. Neither Christian values, nor the pope, nor any European institution, could stop the creation of the death camps. Only an equally compelling firepower put an end to them, which brings us to the black logic of power.

In 1941 Churchill is reported to have said, "A crime is being committed for which we have no name." Now we do. The Holocaust has the dubious distinction of being an historic first. If we wish to know what a technocratic state which worships industrialism, efficiency, technology and medical experimentation, what a scientific civic entity freed from the confines of religious precepts, conscience, ethics, or moral considerations, in short the world envisioned by the nineteenth century physiologists, Magendie, Bernard, Paul Bert, Leon Le Fort, would be like, we have the model.

Is the Holocaust unique? Pray that it is.

But even if it is, even if thismodel is not repeated again, we face now one of the most insidious aspects of modern warfare: the possibilities of chemical, nuclear, or biological warfare. In the United States, about thirty percent of experiments on animals are done for the purpose of developing these kinds of war methods. Modern war may come to us courtesy of several million animals who have been nuked, chemically burned, gassed, irradiated, poisoned, and stricken with typhus, anthrax, small pox, etc. Animals and humans have crossed each others' paths throughout history, but animals today have become the testing grounds not only for our diseases, but for our weapons of choice and what is done to animals, particularly in this industrialized age, is often later done to human beings. To an appreciable extent, in our warfare and biological assault on human nature, the modern world has been ushered in on the backs of animals. The future may hold fearsome deaths in store for us because of the dispersal of weapons throughout the world, the ability to use nuclear, chemical and biological warfare in ever more mobile containers which may spread terrorism to the point of destroying the state as we know it and creating an anarchy of violence everywhere. In such a future animal suffering will cross the path of human history in its usual invisible trajectory, but their histories still do not fit into each other, nor into the history of the Holocaust like interchangeable units. It is not the Jew's body only that is coveted: it is also his immortal soul. The Mormons undertook the vast task of posthumously converting the Jews who died in the Holocaust to Christianity---working to fulfill Peter the Venerable's dream. In our society no hunter or trapper seeks the soul of the animals he kills.

The narrator in the novel, *Black Dogs* by Ian McEwan discovers that Jews are not named in the record of those who died in the concentration camp of Majdanek. "So many hundreds of thousands of Poles, Lithuanians, Russians, French, British, and Americans had died there," but the Jew is obliterated from the record, relegated again to the detritus of history, even in death. Anti-Semitism is not only an historical phenomenon, it is meta-historical. As Ian McEwan writes, it is "a disease of the imagination and a living peril, a barely conscious connivance with evil."

Acknowledgements

The brains of insightful people are among the greatest gifts one can receive. The list of writers to whom I owe the formation of my mind concerning the plight of animals in the modern world is far too long for me to cite here; and the names of authors who have shaped my understanding of anti-Semitism is equally long. I list here only the authors and books whom I have quoted in this work: Diane Ackerman, *A Natural Hiistory of the Senses* (Random House, 1990); Guido Ceronetti, *The Silence of The Body,* trans. Michael Moore (Farrar, Strauss and Giroux, 1993); C. David Coats, *Old MacDonald's Factory Farm* Farm (Continuum, 1989); Karen Davis, *Prisoned Chicken, Poisoned Eggs: An Inside Look at The Modern Poultry Business,* Book Publishing Co., 1996; Mary Douglas, *Purity and Danger* (Routledge, 1996); Gail Eisnitz, *Slaughterhouse* (Prometheus Books, 1997; James M. Glass, *Life Unworthy of Life* (Basic Books, 1997); Ted Kerasote, *Bloodties : Nature, Culture, and the Hunt* (Random House, 1993); Albert Leffingwell, *An Ethical Problem: Sidelights Upon Scientific Experiments on Man and Animals* (G. Bell and Sons, 1916); Julia Kristeva, *Powers of Horror, An Essay on Abjection,* trans. Leon S. Roudiz (Columbia University Press, 1982); Julia Kristeva, *Strangers To Ourselves* (Columbia University Press, 1994); Besant K. Lal, "Hindu Perspectives on the Use of Animals In Science," *Animal Sacrifices: Religious Perspectives on the Use of Animals In Science,* ed. Tom Regan (Temple University Press, 1986); Dominique Iogna-Pratt,

Order and Exclusion: Cluny and Christendom Face Heresy, Judaism, and Islam (1000-1150) (Cornell University Press, 1998; George L. Moss, *The Crisis of German Ideology: Intellectual Origins of The Third Reich* (Grosset and Dunlap, 1964); George L. Moss, *Nazi Culture: Intellectual, Cultural and Social Life In The Third Reich* (Grosset and Dunlap, 1966); Susan Sontag, *Regarding The Pain of Others* (Farrar, Strauss and Giroux, 2003); Marjorie Spiegel, *The Dreaded Comparison: Human And Animal Slavery* (New Society Publishers, 1988); John Vyvyan, *In Pity and In Anger: A Study of The Use of Animals In Science,* and *The Dark Face of Science* (Micah Publications, 1988); E. Westacott, *A Century of Vivisection and Anti-Viviection* (C.W. Daniel Company, Ltd., 1949).

Regretfully, I also list: Claude Bernard, *An Introduction to the Study of Experimental Medicine,* Trans. H.C. Greene (Dover Publications, 1957)

.